The Gospel of Thomas

The Gospel of Thomas

Newly presented to bring out the meaning, with Introductions Paraphrases and Notes, by Hugh McGregor Ross

Calligraphy by John Blamires

FOURTH EDITION

WATKINS PUBLISHING
LONDON

This edition published in the UK in 2006 by
Watkins Publishing, Sixth Floor, Castle House,
75–76 Wells Street, London W1T 3QH
Distributed in the USA and Canada by Publishers Group West

First edition published in 1987 by Sessions of York
Reprinted 1987
Second Edition published in 1991 by Element Books,
Shaftesbury
Third Edition published in 2002 by Watkins Publishing Ltd

1 3 5 7 9 10 8 6 4 2
Calligraphy by John Blamires, Brighouse

Typeset by Alpha Studio, Stroud
Plantin font 11 point on 13
Special Greek and Coptic words by Linotype, Cheltenham
Cover design by 3+Co. (www.threeandco.com)

Printed and bound in Great Britain

Library of Congress Cataloging in Publication data available

ISBN 1 84293 184 9
www.watkinspublishing.com

The author may be reached at Didymos Thomas Books,
Simmondley, Painswick, Stroud, Glos. GL6 6XA, England.

Contents

	page
Foreword	1
Introduction	3
The Primary Presentation	9
The Paraphrases—	
Introduction to the Paraphrases	70
The Paraphrases themselves	73
The Notes	89
References and Acknowledgements	119

Foreword

This translation of the Gospel of Thomas has stood the test of time, being first made available in 1981. However a feature of the Gospel is that it has the power to release the inner meanings of its sayings by insights that spontaneously come to mind over many years. These do not come by punditry or study. These new insights have to be reflected in subtle small changes in the translation. This fourth edition has been fully updated to incorporate them.

From the start the aim has been to make this Gospel available in a form as free as possible from words, phrases or ideas derived from other traditions. It is a direct translation from the Coptic and Greek of the ancient document discovered in Egypt. The translation has benefited from conversations with the late Professor Guilles Quispel. He was the first to identify the Gospel of Thomas and the first to publish it. It has also taken full advantage of the many detailed contributions derived from the philological skill of Phillip de Suarez and the insights of the other French scholars of l'Association Métanoïa. This permits the choice of English words that carry the most appropriate nuance of meaning.

Together with the Paraphrases or more liberal renderings of some difficult sayings, and the many Notes on particular words or phrases, a most meaningful, insightful and helpful translation is provided.

The presentation of the sayings in short phrases follows the practice established by the scholars of l'Association Métanoïa. This reflects a cardinal feature of the speech of Jesus which, except for the Lord's Prayer, has been lost in the Gospels of the Bible. These phrases simulate the cadences and structure of spoken words, especially that of the original Semitic thought. They can suggest the rhythm and emphasis, making use of the punctuation that has been added. You will find it beneficial to read these phrases aloud, giving a natural emphasis, and allowing plenty of time for the meaning of the words to be absorbed. Likewise, benefit will result from copying out in longhand those logia that particularly appeal to you.

Another unique feature is the use of fine hand-drawn calligraphy for all Jesus' words. On the one hand this conveys an affinity with the ancient manuscript from which this translation is derived, and on the other hand makes clear the text contributed by the author which is all set in printers' type.

The Gospel of Thomas was first introduced to the Western world by Guilles Quispel and his colleagues. It was followed soon after by the scholars of l'Association Métanoïa but their work did not appear in the English language. For many years other Biblical scholars or theologians could not risk their professional careers by supporting it. Although scholarly debate still continues, an entirely different scenario has now developed. With the increasing availability of the internet a great community of people is growing up who seek to find out what the Gospel has to offer. They are finding for themselves that an authentic record has been made available to us of sayings by Jesus. It is apparent that some of these were given when Jesus was speaking on public occasions, while others were captured by the disciple Thomas from conversations between Jesus and his immediate followers.

It is from this background of the mission of Jesus to present his awareness of spiritual Truth as a travelling minister, either to the crowds or to people by the wayside or during conversations with the men and women who accompanied him, that you can best appreciate the sayings in this translation.

In the website at www.gospelofthomas.info you will find much to complement this book.

Introduction

The manuscript of the Gospel of Thomas was dug up in 1945 by two peasants in the valley of the Upper Nile, Egypt, while they were seeking fertilizer for their fields. It was one book out of fifty-two, now called the Nag Hammâdi Library, which had been put in a tall jar, the lid sealed with bitumen, and hidden in the sands under a corner of a great boulder at the foot of the cliffs that here define the valley of the Nile.

It is clear that these books constituted treasures of a non-orthodox Christian monastery. During the third and fourth centuries A.D. certain churches, claiming they represented orthodoxy and being the forerunners of the present Western Christian and Eastern Orthodox Churches, were gaining an ascendancy over others. By the third century we hear of this Gospel being branded as heretical, a condemnation that was reiterated later. Thus in the first half of the fourth century the monks in such monasteries were instructed to destroy all books except those officially approved. Those at Nag Hammâdi would have been aware of persecutions that had fallen on others deemed non-orthodox, and must have buried those books as a final homage to the records of beliefs they owned.

Further adventures befell the books after they were found. There are reports of sudden deaths, blood feuds and the frightened mother of the two peasants burning some of the books. Others involved were a Coptic priest, a camel driver, a one-eyed outlaw and dealers in antiquities in various continents. Then there were the national authorities, UNESCO and, not least, scholars who in their covetousness hugged parts of the Library close to their chests in order to be the first to publish them. Now they are out in the open, the old manuscripts are in a Cairo museum, and reproductions are in several Western libraries.

Notwithstanding those hazards, this Gospel survived even greater ones. For over sixteen hundred years it has remained intact, no-one has got at it to modify or up-date it to whatever were the latest prevalent ideas. Even more important, our copy lay unmolested until such time as the established Churches had lost the power to be able to subdue it. It has always been, and still is, unacceptable to ecclesiastical authorities and theologians, if only because it undermines their function and power, and runs counter to many of their doctrines.

The Gospel of Thomas is very different from the other books in the Nag Hammâdi Library, in part due to its form— claiming to be a set of sayings of Jesus, called logia—but chiefly because of its spiritual significance and power. What we have is the record of the Teaching of a Master, with very little coloration or dilution. Scholars can identify that it was first written in Greek—and a very fragmentary alternative version in Greek was discovered in 1898 (the Oxyrhyncus manuscript); the copy we now have is written in Coptic, an Egyptian language influenced by Greek and written with the Greek alphabet, together with a significant number of Greek words. It is virtually complete; the few missing words can be supplied by scholars, and in no case vitally affect the meaning. Because the Egyptian scribe filled out the final line with little symbols it is clear that ours is a complete copy of the version he had before him.

The form of the text is a set of sayings, each given as a

4

series of phrases. These sayings each have an outer and one or more inner meanings. They are expressed in symbolic language, such that on finding the inner meanings they can speak directly to the Being of the seeker. Their wording is concise and precise, and when the inner meanings have been found it may be noted that in general none of the words can be changed without lessening the import—one of the criteria of the sayings of a Master. This in turn is one factor in their authenticity, for there is no evidence whatever from that time and place of a Teacher of greater spiritual capability than Jesus. Some people find that these sayings have a self-authenticating quality.

This Teaching is dealing with aspects of Truth from a very high level. It is inevitable therefore that many passages in it will be difficult. There is a strangeness; from the recorded dialogues with disciples and bystanders it is apparent that it was so to the original hearers, and so it is for us. It will be necessary to ponder on these sayings to get out their meanings. But what is certain is that the original author, whether Jesus or not, was a Master seeking to take his hearers or readers to this higher level. It is the present writer's objective merely to assist the modern reader to find what is in this Teaching, so that he may apply it to his own life. To this end the text of the old manuscript is translated and presented with as little coloration as possible, and is supplemented by more liberal Paraphrases and a series of Notes to help bring out the meanings.

Experience in presenting this Teaching has demonstrated that persons attached to any of the established Christian Churches may have difficulty in responding to it. The doctrines and dogmas of those seem to present barriers. After all, the Master was speaking before any of those great Churches were made by men, speaking to people whose thinking and presuppositions were not coloured by their

5

doctrines. On the other hand much in this Teaching will be found to be deeply harmonious with elements in other great spiritual traditions, especially those of the East. Therefore this volume may be more likely to appeal to those who have moved in those directions, or to others wandering in some wilderness.

Many of the people to whom the Master was speaking were of the Hebrew religion, and we find him using some of their ideas and phrases to help them understand. But for those hearers much more emphasis is placed on presenting something that was new to them. Others to whom he was speaking —nine tenths of the whole population of his time and country—were of Hellenistic background, indigenous people who had absorbed a rustic or popular form of the Greek civilization. So we also find concepts and phrases that would be easy for them. In particular, this would account for the Gospel having been written in Greek.

This Gospel became the primary scripture of a Church that spread across from Egypt, through Palestine to Syria and perhaps beyond. Some of the literature it developed has a deep mystical content. It flourished for five or six centuries until it was extinguished by the more powerful orthodox Churches.

This Teaching claims to have been transmitted by the apostle Didymos Judas Thomas. His birth name was Jewish and Didymos and Thomas, both meaning 'twin', must have been given by the other disciples in recognition of his spiritual affinity to the Master. There are strong living traditions that by 52 A.D. Thomas had begun to set up a Church, still existing, in South India. The only viable conclusion is that he committed the Teaching to writing before that date.

The Teaching here is directed towards the ultimate experience within. This cannot be defined or described by means of words. However, names need to be used even though they cannot do more than serve as pointers. Truth or Ultimate

Reality are instances. In this text several different pointer-names are used: the All or the One come from a Greek idiom, and we may conclude were spoken when the Master was addressing Hellenistic people; the Kingdom or the Father come from the Hebrew tradition and may have been used when such followers were being spoken to. It is one sign of authenticity that such variations have not been smoothed over.

In the Greek philosophical idiom, which we in the West have inherited, it is normal to start any book from some very basic elementary criteria, then gradually to build up an argument or structure, and ultimately come to the conclusions. Recall one's school-days with Euclid's geometry. In the Oriental idiom, on the other hand, the author ponders long on what he wishes to present, refines and distils it, and starts his book with it. The rest of the book may be an expansion of the basic themes, and explanations to help the reader come to an understanding of the initial statements.

The Gospel of Thomas is in this respect Oriental. It may have been something to do with the way in which the apostle Thomas—who certainly had a profound grasp of what he was writing about—selected and marshalled the sayings of his Master which he wished to transmit to posterity. The consequence is that the objectives of the Teaching appear—in very concise form—in the first two pages. This is the Place to which the Master is attempting to take the seeker for spiritual Truth. Starting from a poverty, which is also referred to later as a blindness, darkness or drunkenness, the aim is to come to Know one's inner Self—reciprocal to the Kingdom or the All. This attainment is associated with a dynamic tranquillity—called "a movement with a repose"—from which flows happiness, joy or bliss. The word 'happy' is one of the most frequently occurring in this Teaching.

The meaning of that objective, very simple even if vastly profound and person-changing, is expanded upon subsequently.

Furthermore, the following sayings express, always in symbolic form, the *means* whereby the objective may be attained. In doing this several additional and very important concepts are introduced.

It is prudent therefore to ponder on those two pages, and make good use of the Notes that have been provided. And from time to time refer back to those initial pages, to make sure one is keeping on the right track and gaining greater awareness of their significance.

It has been said that this Teaching can lead to answers for the great questions of life. When one of those comes to mind, it is suggested that the Teaching should be scanned (making use of the Paraphrases) for sayings that might relate to it. Then those sayings be written out and placed where they may be seen from time to time. It is possible that an answer will grow out of them.

The themes in this Introduction, intentionally brief so as not to detract from the Master's Teaching itself, are developed more fully in a series of essays, published as a companion volume to this one. * Their aim is to assist the contemporary seeker to understand the background of this Gospel and its provenance, and to appreciate some of the salient features of that Teaching.

The Gospel of Thomas is not to be read in a rush, as a modern text or this Introduction. Instead, each logion or sometimes even just a few phrases together, needs to be dwelt upon, giving time for its meaning to be revealed and to penetrate. Perhaps a particular use would be for each to be a centre, a focus, for contemplation.

Such words, given by a Master, may have a germinal power. By nurturing them, they may come forth from their hiding and, serving as pointers, grow to have a living quality.

* *Thirty Essays on the Gospel of Thomas*, Hugh McGregor Ross, 1990, Element Books.

The Gospel of Thomas

These are the hidden logia
which the living Jesus spoke
and Didymos Judas Thomas recorded.

1 $_{4N}^{P}$

1 And he said:
2 He who finds the inner meaning of these logia
3 will not taste death.

2 2N
Jesus said:
1 Let him who seeks not cease from seeking
2 until he finds;
3 and when he finds,
4 he will be turned around;
5 and when he is turned around,
6 he will marvel,
7 and he shall reign over the All.

1 Jesus said:

2 If those who guide your Being say to you:

3 "Behold the Kingdom is in the heaven,"

4 then the birds of the sky will precede you;

5 if they say to you: "It is in the sea",

6 then the fish will precede you.

7 But the Kingdom is in your centre

8 and is about you.

9 When you Know your Selves

10 then you will be Known,

11 and you will be aware that you are

12 the sons of the Living Father.

13 But if you do not Know yourselves

14 then you are in poverty,

15 and you are the poverty.

4

1 Jesus said:
2 The man old in days will not hesitate
3 to ask a little child of seven days
4 about the Place of Life,
5 and he will live,
6 for many who are first shall become last
7 and they shall be a single One.

5

1 Jesus said:
2 Know Him who is before your face,
3 and what is hidden from you shall be revealed
to you:
4 for there is nothing hidden that shall not be
manifest.

6

1 His disciples questioned, they said to him:
2 Do you wish that we should fast?
3 And in which way should we pray?
4 Should we give alms?
5 And what diet should we observe?
6 Jesus said:
7 Do not lie,
8 and do not do what you dislike,
9 for all things are revealed before heaven.
10 For there is nothing hidden that shall not be
manifest,
11 and there is nothing concealed
12 that shall remain without being revealed.

7 $^{P}_{2N}$

1 Jesus said:
2 Happy is the lion which the man will eat,
3 and the lion will become man;
4 and abominated is the man whom the lion
will eat,
5 and the lion will become man.

8 N

1 And he said:

2 The Man is like a wise fisherman

3 who cast his net into the sea;

4 he drew it up from the sea full of small fish.

5 Amongst them,

6 he found a large fine fish.

7 That wise fisherman, he cast all the small fish
down to the bottom of the sea,

8 he chose the large fish without trouble.

9 He who has ears to hear let him hear!

1 Jesus said:

2 Behold, the sower went out.

3 He filled his hand and threw.

4 Some seeds indeed fell on the road;

5 the birds came and plundered them.

6 Others fell on the rock

7 and did not take root in the earth

8 nor did they send up their heads to the sky.

9 And others fell on thorn trees;

10 these choked the seeds

11 and the worms ate them.

12 Others fell on tilled earth,

13 which brought forth good produce to the sky;

14 it bore sixty per measure

15 even one hundred and twenty per measure.

10

1 Jesus said:

2 I have cast a fire upon the world,

3 and behold, I guard it

4 until it is ablaze.

11 $\frac{P}{2}$ N

1 Jesus said:

2 This heaven will pass away,

3 and that which is above it will pass away,

4 and the dead do not live,

5 and the living will not die.

6 In the days you fed on what is dead,

7 you made of that, the living.

8 When you are in the Light

9 what will you do!

10 On the day you were One,

11 you created the two;

12 but then being two,

13 what will you do?

12 N

1 The disciples said to Jesus:

2 We realize that you will go away from us;

3 who is it that will be great over us?

4 Jesus said to them:

5 Whatever place you have come to,

6 you will go to James the righteous,

7 because of whom heaven and earth came
into being.

1 Jesus said to his disciples:
2 Make a comparison to me
3 and tell me whom I resemble.
4 Simon Peter said to him:
5 You resemble a righteous angel.
6 Matthew said to him:
7 You resemble a wise man, a philosopher.
8 Thomas said to him:
9 Master, my mouth will absolutely not permit
10 me to say you resemble anyone.
11 Jesus said:
12 I am not your Master;
13 because you have drunk,
14 you have become enlivened from the bubbling
   spring
15 which I have made to gush out.
16 He took him aside,
17 and spoke three logia to him.
18 Now, when Thomas had returned to his
   companions,
19 they questioned him:
20 What did Jesus say to you?
21 Thomas said to them:

(13)

22 If I tell you one of the logia that he said to me,
23 you will take up stones
24 and throw them against me;
25 and fire will come forth from the stones
26 and burn you up.

14 P

1 Jesus said to them:
2 If you fast
3 you will beget a sin to yourselves,
4 and if you pray
5 you will be condemned,
6 and if you give alms
7 you will do harm to your spirits.
8 And as you go into every land
9 and wander in the countryside,
10 if they receive you,
11 eat what they set before you,
12 heal the sick amongst them.
13 For what goes into your mouth
14 will not defile you,
15 but what comes out of your mouth,
16 that is what will defile you.

15 N

1 Jesus said:
2 When you behold
3 Him who was not begotten of woman,
4 prostrate yourselves upon your face
5 and worship him;
6 that one is your Father.

16$^{P}_{2N}$

1 Jesus said:
2 Perhaps men think
3 that I have come to cast concord upon
the world,
4 and they do not realize
5 that I have come to cast separations upon
the earth,
6 fire, sword, strife.
7 For there will be five in a home,
8 three will be against two,
9 and two against three,
10 the father against the son,
11 and the son against the father,
12 and they shall stand boldly, being 'loners'.

17

1 Jesus said:
2 I will give you what no eye has seen,
3 and what no ear has heard,
4 and what no hand has touched,
5 and what has not arisen in the heart of man.

18 ²ᴾₙ

1 The disciples said to Jesus:
2 Tell us in what way our end will be.
3 Jesus said:
4 Have you therefore discerned the beginning
5 in order that you seek after the end ?
6 For in the Place where the beginning is,
7 there will be the end.
8 Happy is he who will stand boldly at the
beginning,
9 he shall Know the end,
10 and shall not taste death.

19 $^P_{2N}$

1 Jesus said:
2 Happy is he who already was
3 before he is.
4 If you become my disciples
5 and hear my logia,
6 these stones will minister to you.
7 'For you have five trees in Paradise
8 which are unchanged in summer or winter
9 and their leaves do not fall away.
10 He who Knows them
11 shall not taste death.

20 $_N$

1 The disciples said to Jesus:
2 Tell us, what is the Kingdom of the heavens
like?
3 He said to them:
4 It is like a grain of mustard,
5 smaller than all seeds;
6 but when it falls on the tilled earth,
7 it sends forth a large stem
8 and becomes a shelter for the birds of the sky.

1 Mary said to Jesus:
2 Whom do your disciples resemble?
3 He said:
4 They resemble small children
5 dwelling in a field
6 which is not theirs.
7 When the owners of the field come,
8 they will say
9 "Release to us our field."
10 'They strip off their outward façade before them
11 to release it to them
12 and to give back their field to them.
13 For this reason I say:
14 If the owner of the house is aware
15 that the thief is coming,
16 he will stay awake before he comes
17 and will not allow the thief
18 to tunnel into his house of his Kingdom
19 to carry away his goods.
20 But you, already watch the world,
21 prepare for action with great strength
22 lest the robbers should find a way
23 to come to you;

(21)

24 because the advantage that you expect,

25 they will find.

26 Let there be in your centre

27 a man who is understanding!

28 When the produce ripened

29 he came in haste, his sickle in his hand,

30 he reaped it.

31 He who has ears to hear let him hear!

1 Jesus saw children who were being suckled..

2 He said to his disciples:

3 These children who are being suckled are like

4 those who enter the Kingdom.

5 'They said to him:

6 Shall we then, being children,

7 enter the Kingdom?

8 Jesus said to them:

9 When you make the two One,

10 and you make the inner as the outer,

11 and the outer as the inner,

12 and the above as the below,

13 so that you will make the male and the female

14 into a single One,

15 in order that the male is not made male

16 nor the female made female:

17 when you make eyes into an eye,

18 and a hand into a hand,

19 and a foot into a foot,

20 and even an image into an image,

21 then shall you enter the Kingdom.

23

1 Jesus said:
2 I will choose you, one out of a thousand,
3 and two out of ten thousand,
4 and they shall stand boldly being a single One.

24 N

1 His disciples said:
2 Show us the Place where you are,
3 because it is necessary for us to seek after it.
4 He said to them:
5 He who has ears let him hear:
6 There is Light
7 at the centre of a man of Light,
8 and he illumines the whole world.
9 If he does not shine,
10 there is darkness.

25

1 Jesus said:
2 Love your brother even as your own soul,
3 guard him
4 even as the pupil of your eye.

26

1 Jesus said:
2 The mote that is in your brother's eye
3 you see,
4 but the beam that is in your own eye
5 you see not.
6 When you cast the beam out of your eye,
7 then you will see clearly
8 to cast the mote out of your brother's eye.

27 $^P_{2N}$

1 If you abstain not from the world,
2 you will not find the Kingdom;
3 if you keep not the sabbath as sabbath,
4 you will not behold the Father.

28 $_{2N}$

1 Jesus said:
2 I stood boldly in the midst of the world
3 and I manifested to them in the flesh.
4 I found them all drunk;
5 I found none among them athirst,
6 and my soul was afflicted for the sons of men
7 because they are blind in their heart
8 and they do not see
9 that empty they came into the world
10 and that empty they seek to go out of the
world again,
11 except that now they are drunk.
12 When they shake off their wine,
13 then they will transform their Knowing.

29 P

1 Jesus said:
2 If the flesh has come into being because
                                 of the spirit,
3 it is a marvel;
4 but if the spirit has come into being because
                                 of the body,
5 it is a marvel of marvels.
6 But I, I marvel at this:
7 about this great wealth
8 put in this poverty.

30 P

1 Jesus said:
2 The place where there are three gods,
3 they are gods;
4 where there are two or one,
5 I myself am with him.

31

1 Jesus said:
2 No prophet is accepted in his own village;
3 no physician heals those who recognize him.

32

1 Jesus said:
2 A city built on a high mountain
3 and made strong
4 cannot fall,
5 nor can it be hidden.

33

1 Jesus said:
2 What you will hear in one ear
3 and in the other Ear,
4 that proclaim from your housetops.
5 For no one lights a lamp
6 and puts it under a bowl,
7 nor does he put it in a hidden place,
8 but he sets it on the lamp stand
9 in order that everyone who goes in and
comes out
10 may see its light.

34 N

1 Jesus said:
2 If a blind man guides the Being of a blind man,
3 both of them fall to the bottom of a pit.

35 P
N

1 Jesus said:
2 It is not possible
3 for one to enter the house of the strong man
4 and take it by force
5 unless he binds his hands;
6 then he will plunder his house.

36

1 Jesus said:
2 Have no care, from morning until evening
3 and from evening until morning,
4 for what you will put on.

37 ^P_N

1 His disciples said:
2 On which day will you be manifest to us
3 and on which day will we behold you?
4 Jesus said:
5 When you strip yourselves of your shame,
6 and take your garments
7 and put them under your feet
8 even as little children,
9 and you trample them;
10 then shall you behold the Son
11 of Him who is living,
12 and you shall not fear.

38

1 Jesus said:
2 Many times have you longed to hear these
logia
3 which I say to you,
4 and you have no other
5 from whom to hear them.
6 There will be days
7 when you seek after me
8 and you will not find me.

39

1 Jesus said:
2 The Pharisees and the scribes
3 took the keys of Knowledge,
4 and they hid them.
5 Neither did they enter,
7 nor did they allow
6 those who wished to enter.
8 But you, become prudent as serpents
9 and innocent even as doves.

40 P N

1 Jesus said:
2 A vine was planted without the Father
3 and, being not made firm,
4 it will be pulled up by its roots
5 and perish.

41 ^P

1 Jesus said:
2 He who has in his hand,
3 to him shall be given;
4 and he who does not have,
5 even the little that he has
6 shall be taken from him.

42 ^P_N

1 Jesus said:
2 Become yourselves, while passing by.

43

1 His disciples said to him:
2 Who are you that you should say these things
to us?

3 [Jesus said to them:] From what I say to you,
4 are you not aware who I am?
5 But you, you were even as the Jews:
6 for they love the tree,
7 they dislike its fruit;
8 and they love the fruit,
9 they dislike the tree.

44

1 Jesus said:
2 He who blasphemes against the Father,
3 it shall be forgiven him,
4 and he who blasphemes against the Son,
5 it shall be forgiven him;
6 but he who blasphemes against the pure Spirit,
7 it shall not be forgiven him, neither on earth
nor in heaven.

45

1 Jesus said:
2 Grapes are not harvested from thorn trees
3 nor are figs gathered from thistles,
4 for these give no fruit.
5 A good man brings forth good from his
                                     storehouse,
6 a bad man brings forth ill
7 from his wicked storehouse
8 which is in his heart,
9 and he speaks ill:
10 for out of the abundance of the heart
11 he brings forth ill.

46 ^P_{2N}

1 Jesus said:
2 From Adam until John the Baptist,
3 among the children begotten of women
4 there is none higher than John the Baptist,
5 such that his vision will not be blurred.
6 But I have said:
7 He who amongst you becomes as a child
8 shall know the Kingdom,
9 and he shall be higher than John.

1 Jesus said:

2 It is impossible

3 for a man to mount two horses,

4 for him to stretch two bows;

5 and it is impossible

6 for a servant to serve two masters,

7 otherwise he will honour the one

8 and offend the other.

9 Let a man drink old wine

10 and now he longs to drink new wine.

11 And new wine is not poured

12 into old wineskins,

13 lest they should burst;

14 and old wine is not poured

15 into a new wineskin,

16 lest this be spoiled.

17 An old patch is not sewn

18 on to a new garment,

19 because there would be a division.

48 P
N

1 Jesus said:
2 If two make peace with each other
3 in this single house,
4 they will say to the mountain
5 "Move away"
6 and it shall move.

49 P
2N

1 Jesus said:
2 Happy are the 'loners' and the chosen
3 for you shall find the Kingdom.
4 Because you are from the heart of it,
5 you shall return there again.

1 Jesus said:

2 If they say to you:

3 "Where are you from?"

4 say to them:

5 "We came from the Light

6 there, where the Light was,

7 by itself.

8 It stood boldly

9 and manifested itself in their image".

10 If they say to you:

11 "Who are you?"

12 say:

13 "We are His sons

14 and we are the chosen of the Living Father."

15 If they question you:

16 "What is the sign of your Father in you?"

17 say to them:

18 "It is a movement with a repose."

51 N

1 His disciples said to him:
2 On which day
3 will the repose of the dead come about?
4 And on which day
5 will the new world come?
6 He said to them:
7 What you expect has come
8 but you, you recognize it not.

52 N

1 His disciples said to him:
2 Twenty-four prophets spoke in Israel
3 and they all spoke about your nature.
4 He said to them:
5 You have ignored Him who is living before
you,
6 and you have spoken about the dead.

53 P N

1 His disciples said to him:
2 Is circumcision beneficial or not?
3 He said to them:
4 If it were beneficial,
5 their father would beget them circumcised
                              from their mother.
6 But the true circumcision, in spirit,
7 gives the ultimate benefit.

54

1 Jesus said:
2 Happy are the poor,
3 for yours is the Kingdom of the heavens.

55 P N

1 Jesus said:
2 He who does not turn away from his father
                              and his mother
3 will not be able to become my disciple,
4 and he who does not turn away from his
                              brothers and sisters
5 and does not bear his cares in my way,
6 will not be worthy of me.

56 ^P

1 Jesus said:
2 He who has known the world
3 has found a corpse;
4 and he who has found a corpse
5 of him the world is not worthy.

57 3N

1 Jesus said:
2 The Kingdom of the Father is like a man
3 who owned good seed.
4 His enemy came by night,
5 he sowed weeds among the good seed.
6 The man did not allow the labourers to pull
up the weeds;
7 he said to them: lest perhaps you should go,
8 saying "we will pull up the weeds,"
9 and you pull up the wheat with it.
10 For on the day of the harvest
11 the weeds will appear;
12 they will be pulled up and will be burned.

58 ^P

1 *Jesus said:*
2 *Happy is the man who has toiled,*
3 *he has found the Life.*

59

1 *Jesus said:*
2 *Look upon Him who is living*
3 *as long as you live,*
4 *lest you should die*
5 *and you should seek to see Him;*
6 *and you would not be able to see.*

60

1 They saw a Samaritan,

2 carrying a lamb,

3 going into Judea.

4 He said to his disciples:

5 Why does this man carry the lamb about?

6 They said to him:

7 In order that he may kill it and eat it.

8 He said to them:

9 As long as it is alive

10 he will not eat it,

11 but only if he kills it

12 and it becomes a corpse.

13 They said:

14 Otherwise he will not be able to do it.

15 He said to them:

16 You yourselves, seek after a Place for yourselves

17 within Repose,

18 lest you become corpses

19 and be eaten.

1 Jesus said:

2 Two will rest there on a couch:

3 one will die, the other will live.

4 Salome said:

5 Who are you, man?

6 Is it even as he from the One

7 that you reclined on my couch

8 and ate at my table?

9 Jesus said to her:

10 I am He who is,

11 from Him who is the same;

12 what belongs to my Father was given to me.

13 Salome said: I myself am your disciple.

14 Jesus added: Because of that I say this:

15 When he is emptied

16 he will be filled with Light;

17 but when he is divided

18 he will be filled with darkness.

1 Jesus said:
2 I tell my mysteries
3 to those who are worthy of my mysteries.
4 Whatever your right hand will do,
5 let not your left hand be aware
6 of what it does.

63

1 Jesus said:
2 There was a rich man
3 who had much wealth.
4 He said:
5 I will use my wealth
6 in order that I may sow and reap and plant,
7 and fill my storehouses with produce
8 so that I lack nothing.
9 This was what he thought in his heart;
10 and during that night he died.
11 He who has ears let him hear!

64

1 Jesus said:

2 A man had guests

3 and when he had prepared the dinner

4 he sent his servant to invite the guests.

5 He went to the first

6 and said to him:

7 "My master invites you."

8 He said:

9 "I have some money for some traders;

10 they will come to me in the evening.

11 I will go and place orders with them.

12 I ask to be excused from the dinner."

13 He went to another

14 he said to him:

15 "My master invites you."

16 He said to him:

17 "I have bought a house and am requested
                                          for a day.

18 I will not be available."

19 He came to another

20 he said to him:

21 "My master invites you."

22 He said to him:

(64)

23 "My friend is to be married
24 and I am to arrange a feast;
25 I shall not be able to come.
26 I ask to be excused from the dinner."
27 He went to another
28 he said to him:
29 "My master invites you."
30 He said to him:
31 "I have bought a farm.
32 I go to collect the rent.
33 I shall not be able to come,
34 I ask to be excused."
35 'The servant came;
36 he said to his master:
37 "Those whom you have invited to the dinner
        have excused themselves."
38 The master said to his servant:
39 "Go outside to the roads,
40 bring those whom you will find,
41 so that they may dine."
42 Buyers and merchants
43 shall not enter
44 the Place of my Father.

1 He said:

2 A benevolent man had a vineyard.

3 He gave it to husbandmen

4 so that they would work it

5 and he would receive his produce from their hands.

6 He sent his servant

7 in order that the husbandmen would give him

8 the fruit of the vineyard.

9 They laid hold of his servant,

10 they beat him;

11 a little more and they would have killed him.

12 The servant went,

13 he reported to his master.

14 His master said:

15 "Perhaps he did not know them."

16 He sent another servant;

17 the husbandmen beat him also.

18 Then the owner sent his son;

19 he said:

20 "Perhaps they will respect my son."

21 Because those husbandmen realized

22 that he was the heir to the vineyard,

23 they seized him, they killed him.

24 He who has ears let him hear!

66

1 Jesus said:
2 Show me the stone
3 which the builders have rejected:
4 it is that, the corner-stone.

67 $^{P}_{N}$

1 Jesus said:
2 He who understands the All,
3 but lacking himself
4 lacks everything.

68 N

1 Jesus said:
2 Happy are you
3 when you are disliked
4 and you are pursued;
5 and no Place will be found there,
6 where you have been pursued in the heart.

69 P

1 Jesus said:
2 Happy are they
3 who have been pursued in their heart.
4 It is they
5 who have known the Father in Truth.
6 Happy are they who are hungry,
7 so that the belly of those who desire shall
                                          be satisfied.

70 P
      N

1 Jesus said:
2 When you bring forth that in yourselves,
3 this which is yours will save you;
4 if you do not have that in yourselves,
5 this which is not yours in you will kill you.

71 P
      N

1 Jesus said:
2 I will overturn this house,
3 and no one will be able to build it again.

72

1 A man said to him:
2 Tell my brothers
3 to divide my father's possessions with me.
4 He said to him:
5 Oh man, who made me a divider?
6 He turned to his disciples,
7 he said to them:
8 Is it that I am a divider?

73

1 Jesus said:
2 The harvest is indeed great,
3 but the labourers are few.
4 Entreat, therefore, the Lord
5 to send labourers to the harvest.

74 P

1 He said:
2 Lord, there are many around the well
3 but none in the well.

75 $^P_{2N}$

1 *Jesus said:*
2/3 *There are many standing at the door,*
4 *but the 'loners' are they*
5 *who shall enter the marriage place.*

76

1 *Jesus said:*
2 *The Kingdom of the Father is like a man, a*
merchant,
3 *who owned merchandise,*
4 *and found a pearl.*
5 *That merchant was wise:*
6 *he sold the merchandise,*
7 *he bought this one single pearl for himself.*
8 *You also, seek after the treasure*
9 *which does not perish,*
10 *which remains in the place*
11 *where no moth comes near to devour,*
12 *and no worm destroys.*

1 Jesus said:

2 I am the Light that is above them all.

3 I am the All.

4 The All comes forth from me,

5 and the All reaches towards me.

6 Cleave the wood, I am there;

7 raise the stone,

8 and you shall find me there.

1 Jesus said:

2 Why did you come forth to the country?

3 To see a reed shaken by the wind

4/5 and to see a man clothed in soft garments?

6 See, your kings and your nobles;

7 these are clothed in soft garments,

8 and they will not be able to Know the Truth.

79 2N

1 A woman from the multitude said to him:
2 Fortunate is the womb that bore you
3 and the breasts that nourished you.
4 He said to her:
5 Fortunate are they who have heard the Logos
                                    of the Father,
6 and have kept it in truth.
7 For there will be days when you will say:
8 Fortunate is the womb that did not conceive
9 and the breasts that did not suckle.

80 P N

1 Jesus said:
2 He who has known the world
3 has found the body;
4 but he who has found the body
5 of him the world is not worthy.

81 P

1 Jesus said:
2 He who has become rich,
3 let him become king;
4 and he who has power,
5 let him renounce it !

82

1 Jesus said:
2 He who is near to me is near to the fire,
3 and he who is far from me is far from the
Kingdom.

83 N

1 Jesus said:
2 The images are manifest to man
3 and the Light that is amongst them is hidden.
4 In the image of the Light of the Father
5 the Light will reveal itself
6 and his image is hidden by his Light.

84 P N

1 Jesus said:
2 In the days you see your resemblance,
3 you rejoice.
4 But when you will see your images
5 that in the beginning were in you,
6 which neither die nor are manifest,
7 oh! how will you bear!

85

1 Jesus said:
2 Adam came into being from a great power
3 and a great richness,
4 and he was not worthy of you;
5 for had he been worthy,
6 he would not have tasted death.

86

1 Jesus said:
2 The foxes have their dens
3 and the birds have their nest,
4 but the Son of man has no place
5 to lay his head and to rest.

87 P

1 Jesus said:
2 Wretched is the body that depends on a body,
3 and wretched is the soul that depends on

these two.

88 N

1 Jesus said:
2 The angels with the prophets will come to you
3 and they will give you what is yours.
4 You also, give what is in your hands
5 to them,
6 and say to yourselves:
7 On which day will they come
8 and receive what is theirs?

89 N

1 Jesus said:
2 Why do you wash the outside of the cup?
3 Do you not understand
4 that He who made the inside
5 is also He who made the outside?

90 N

1 Jesus said:
2 Come to me,
3 for easy is my yoke
4 and my lordship is gentle,
5 and you shall find Repose for yourselves.

91 N

1 They said to him:
2 Tell us who you are
3 so that we may believe in you.
4 He said to them:
5 You scrutinize the face of heaven and earth,
6 and him who is before you
7 you have not Known,
8 and you know not how to probe this revelation.

92 N

1 Jesus said:
2 Seek and you will find.
3 But those things
4 that you asked me in those days
5 I did not tell you then;
6 now I desire to tell them
7 but you do not seek after them.

93 N

1 Give not what is pure to dogs,
2 lest they cast it on the dung-heap.
3 Throw not pearls to swine
4 lest they pollute them.

94 N

1 Jesus said:
2 He who seeks shall find,
3 and to him who knocks it shall be opened.

95 ^P_N

1 Jesus said:
2 If you have money,
3 do not lend at interest,
4 but give it
5 to him who will not return it.

96

1 Jesus said:
2 The Kingdom of the Father is like a woman,
3 who took a little leaven,
4 hid it in dough
5 and of it made large loaves.
6 He who has ears let him hear!

97 P

1 Jesus said:
2 The Kingdom of the Father is like a woman
3 who was carrying a jar full of flour
4 while walking on a long road;
5 the handle of the jar broke
6 the flour streamed out behind her on the road.
7 As she did not know it
8 she could not be troubled by it.
9 When she had reached her house
10 she put the jar on the ground;
11 she found it empty.

98 P

1 Jesus said:
2 The Kingdom of the Father is like a man
3 wishing to kill a giant.
4 He drew the sword in his house,
5 he struck it through the wall
6 in order to be assured that his hand would
                              be confident.
7 Then he slew the giant.

99 N

1 The disciples said to him:
2 Your brothers and your mother are
                                    standing outside.
3 He said to them:
4 Those here who do the wish of my Father
5 they are my brothers and my mother.
6 These are they
7 who shall enter the Kingdom of my Father.

100 N

1 They showed Jesus a gold coin
2 and said to him:
3 Caesar's agents demand taxes from us.
4 He said to them:
5 Give the things of Caesar to Caesar,
6 give the things of God to God,
7 and that which is mine, give to me.

101

1 He who does not turn away from his father
and his mother
2 in my way
3 will not be able to become my disciple;
4 and he who does not love his Father and his
Mother
5 in my way
6 will not be able to become my disciple;
7 for my mother has begotten me
8 but my true Mother gave me Life.

102

1 Jesus said:
2 Woe to them, the Pharisees!
3 For they resemble a dog
4 sleeping in the oxen's manger;
5 for neither does he eat
6 nor does he allow the oxen to eat.

103 ^P_N

1 Jesus said:

2 Happy is the man who knows

3 where and when the robbers will creep in;

4 so that he will arise

5 and gather his strength

6 and prepare for action

7 before they come.

104

1 They said to him:

2 Come and let us pray today and let us fast!

3 Jesus said:

4 What therefore is the sin that I have committed

5 or in what have I been overcome?

6 But when the bridegroom comes forth from
                              the bridal chamber

7 then let them fast and let them pray.

105 ^P

1 Jesus said:

2 He who knows the Father and the Mother,

3 will he be called the son of a harlot?

106 P

1 Jesus said:
2 When you make the two One,
3 you will become Sons of man,
4 and if you say:
5 "Mountain, move away,"
6 it shall move.

107 N

1 Jesus said:
2 'The Kingdom is like a shepherd
3 who owned a hundred sheep.
4 One among them, which was the largest,
                              went astray;
5 he left the ninety-nine,
6· he sought after the one
7 until he found it.
8 When he had toiled,
9 he said to the sheep:
10 I desire you more than the ninety-nine!

108N

1 Jesus said:
2 He who drinks from my mouth
3 shall become as me ;
4 and I myself will become him,
5 and the hidden things shall be manifested.

1093N

1 Jesus said:
2 The Kingdom is like a man
3 who owned in his field a hidden treasure,
4 it being unknown to him.
5 He bequeathed it to his son after he died.
6 The son not knowing of it,
7 took that field
8 and sold it.
9 And he who bought it, came.
10 While ploughing, he found the treasure;
11 he began to lend money at interest
12 to whomsoever he wished.

110

1 Jesus said:
2 He who has found the world
3 and become rich,
4 let him deny the world!

111 [P]

1 Jesus said:
2 The heavens and the earth will roll back
3 before you,
4 and he who is living, from the Living,
5 shall see neither death nor fear,
6 because Jesus says this:
7 He who finds himself,
8 of him the world is not worthy.

112 P/N

1 Jesus said:
2 Woe to the flesh that depends upon the soul!
3 Woe to the soul that depends upon the flesh!

113

1 His disciples said to him:
2 On which day will the Kingdom come?
3 Jesus said: It will not come by expectation.
4 They will not say:
5 "Behold, it is here!"
6 or "Behold, there!"
7 But the Kingdom of the Father is spread out
over the earth
8 and men do not see it.

114 N

1 *Simon Peter said to them:*
2 *Let Mary go out from amongst us,*
3 *because women are not worthy of the Life.*
4 *Jesus said:*
5 *Behold, I will guide her Being,*
6 *in order that I make her male*
7 *that she shall become a living spirit,*
8 *like you males.*
9 *For every woman who makes herself male*
10 *shall enter the Kingdom of the heavens.*

The Gospel according to Thomas

The Paraphrases

Introduction to the Paraphrases

A logion when received, perhaps in contemplation, has the power to raise the recipient to awareness of a facet of Truth. Thus it deals with the inmost region of our Beings, of which we may be unfamiliar even though we must have a sense of it. In order to have this power, logia need to be expressed in symbolic language, for if more specific words were used the reader would be trapped at the level of the mind. Hence these logia may at first seem enigmatic, or in some cases their flexibility may even appear as contradictions.

Experience shows that for each of these logia that may bear differing interpretations it may be of value to have an indication of a meaning that is consistent with the overall content of the Teaching. Thus a degree of homogeneity may be attained, the justification being that all came from a single source. This is what the following Paraphrases aim to supply, although it needs to be emphasized that they cannot be other than an individual interpretation.

The Paraphrases use a term—the ego—that is not in the rendering of the Gospel. It is used here with a different meaning from that used by psychologists. In some spiritual teachings it is referred to as the 'little self', to distinguish it from the real Self.

Other books of the Nag Hammâdi library refer to what is here called the ego, and the concept was familiar in the communities in which this Teaching was treasured. Probably at that time the Teaching was communicated to those seeking Truth by one who had assimilated the meaning of this concept, and in expanding on the various logia it could have been presented.

While the ego can be regarded in its own right, it becomes clearer as a contrast with the real Self. To recognize what is meant by the ego requires fundamental considerations. Each man or woman comprises body, mind and emotions, and a Self over all. Ordinary language reflects this awareness; we say "my body", "my mind and thoughts", "my feelings and emotions". These phrases come entirely naturally to us; we know them to be valid without anyone having to convince us. The point is: who is it who can say "my"? It is the real Self.

The real Self, the true Self are synonyms. So too are Reality, Truth, the Absolute, the Ultimate; and also terms used in this Gospel—the All, One, Unity, the Kingdom, Life, the Living, the Father, Kingdom of the Father, the Father and the Mother, Light, the Pure Spirit, Kingdom of the heavens—all these are as facets on the jewel that is this. The jewel itself is of course beyond the capability of any word or words to describe—parts of something cannot describe the whole.

The ego derives from the mind, the emotions, the body and outward material factors. Being egoistic or selfish, self-opinionated, self-assertive or competitive, possessive, proud, changeable or vacillating, distressed or sad, despairing or fearful, thinking up concepts or doctrines, are manifestations of the ego. Suffering belongs to the ego—it is very important to note that.

Happiness and bliss, peace and repose and tranquillity, certainty and stability and assurance and steadiness, contentment, consideration and generosity, love and beauty, reliance, strength and fearlessness, knowledge, belong to the real Self.

We each naturally have, or grow to have, an ego. It is far more difficult to see it in oneself than in others—one of its tricks. It is the equation of oneself with one's body and mind. Due to the influence of the bodily senses and of the intellect and emotions, it readily becomes dominant. But as the centre of attention is transferred from the ego to the real Self so Truth becomes known.

This transference, in essence, consists in overcoming the *dominance* of the ego. This is best done by first recognizing and accepting the ego, and then concentrating on the positive. If the attention is concentrated on the ego itself, this will merely be strengthened.

It is a mistake to think that this rejection of the ego involves a denigration of worldly activities and interests. No, this release from its dominance is to be distinguished from regarding the body, the mind and emotions, and the outer world as corrupt or sinful. It is entirely possible to admire the highest edifices of the intellect and of science, to wonder at the working of all the parts of the body, to be entranced by artistic or natural things, to treasure all the good things of daily life, and yet to stand one stage removed from them. Seen thus, at their highest these reach up toward the Ultimate.

This transference, this overcoming of the dominance of the ego, may come gradually and easily (logion 97); or it may require persistent effort (logia 37 and 38); or, because the ego can produce innumerable objections to this usurpation of its rôle, it may appear as a powerful man to be slain (logion 98). And it can keep on creeping back at us, like robbers (logion 103).

In the Paraphrases, an asterisk against a phrase indicates that words have been changed or added, relative to the handwritten version.

1 .1   And he said:

 *.2   He or she who finds the inner meaning of these logia

 *.3   will find the Life that is independent of the death
                                                    of the body.

7 .1   The Master said;

 *.2   Happy are the primeval forces that the enlightened
                                        man will assimilate,

 *.3   and they will be integrated and purified by the man;

 *.4   but abominated is the ordinary man consumed
                                            by those forces,

 *.5   and they will constitute that man.

11 .1   The Master said:

* .2, .3   Everything above, being of the world of objects,

.3   will pass away;

* .4   The dead, being in duality, do not live,

* .5   the living, in the Unity, will not die.

* .6   In the days when you fed on the world of objects

.7   you made it alive.

.8   When you come into the light

.9   what will you do!

* .10   On the day when you were One

* .11   you made it duality;

.12   but then being two

.13   what will you do?

14 .1   The Master said to them:

.2   If you fast

*.3   you will do something prejudicial to yourselves,

.4   and if you pray

.5   you will be condemned,

.6   and if you give alms

.7   you will do harm to your spirits.

.8   And as you go into every land

.9   and wander in the countryside,

.10   if they receive you

.11   eat what is set before you,

.12   heal the sick amongst them.

.13   For what goes into your mouth

.14   will not defile you,

.15   but what comes out of your mouth,

*.16   that is what may defile you.

75

16.1 The Master said:

.2 Perhaps men think

.3 that I have come to cast concord upon the world,

.4 and they do not realize

.5 that I have come to cast separations on the world,

.6 fire, sword, strife.

.7 For there will be five in a house,

.8 three will be against two,

.9 and two against three,

.10 the father against the son,

.11 the son against the father,

★.12 and standing in their own strength they will be
willing to be on their own.

18.1 The disciples said to Jesus:

.2 Tell us in what way our end will be.

.3 The Master said:

.4 Have you therefore discerned the beginning

★.5 since you seek after the end?

.6 For in the Place where the beginning is,

.7 there will be the end.

★.8 Happy is he who will stand in his own strength at
the beginning,

.9 he shall know the end,

★.10 and shall be independent of the death of the body.

19.1   The Master said:

*.2   Happy is he who is aware that his earlier original form

*.3   and his present Being are one and the same.

.4   If you become my disciples

.5   and hear my logia,

*.6   even these stones will minister to you.

.7   For you have five trees in Paradise

.8   which are unchanged in summer or winter

.9   and their leaves do not fall away.

.10   He who knows them

*.11   shall be independent of the death of the body.

27*.1   If you do not transcend the world of objects

.2   you will not find the Kingdom;

*.3   if you do not make of the sabbath a true sabbath

.4   you will not behold the Father.

29.1   The Master said:

.2   If the flesh has come into being because of the spirit,

.3   it is a marvel;

.4   but if the spirit has come into being because of the body,

.5   it is a marvel of marvels.

.6   But I, I marvel at this:

*.7   about this great richness of spiritual Truth

*.8   put within this poor world of objects.

30.1   The Master said:

*.2   In the three heavens

*.3   there are merely gods;

*.4   where there is the Father and the Mother,

.5   I myself am with him.

35.1   The Master said:

.2   It is not possible

*.3   for a man to enter the domain of the powerful ego

*.4   and overcome it

*.5   unless he overcomes and restrains that power;

*.6   then he will plunder that domain.

37.1   His disciples said:

.2   On which day will you be manifest to us

.3   and on which day will we behold you?

.4   The Master said:

*.5   When you strip yourselves of your pride and ostentation,

*.6   and take your outward façades

*.7   and treat them as nought

*.8   —even as do little children—

*.9   and, furthermore, scorn and discard them;

*.10,.11 Then shall you behold the living Master,

.12   and you shall not fear.

40.1   *The Master said:*
  *.2   *A life that is founded without the Father*
   .3   *and being not made firm,*
  *.4,.5 *will be uprooted, and perish.*

41.1   *The Master said:*
  *.2   *He who is seeking and has begun to find the Truth,*
   .3   *to him shall be given;*
   .4   *and he who does not have,*
   .5   *even the little that he has*
  *.6   *shall be taken away from him.*

42.1   *The Master said:*
  *.2   *Become your true Selves, as your egos pass away.*

46.1   *The Master said:*
   .2   *From Adam to John the Baptist,*
  *.3   *among the children born of women*
   .4   *there is none higher than John the Baptist,*
  *.5   *such that his vision will have the potential to see Truth.*
   .6   *But I have said:*
   .7   *He who amongst you becomes as a child*
   .8   *shall know the Kingdom,*
   .9   *and he shall be higher than John.*

48.1 The Master said:

.2 If two make peace with each other

*.3 in this single domain,

*.4 they will say to the mountain of distress and trouble

.5 "Move away"

.6 and it shall move.

49.1 The Master said:

*.2 Happy are they who stand in their own strength
 born of finding Oneness, and willing to be separated,

.3 for you shall find the Kingdom.

*.4 Because you are come from the heart of it,

*.5 you shall return there again.

53.1 His disciples said to him:

.2 Is circumcision beneficial or not?

.3 He said to them:

.4 If it were beneficial,

.5 their father would beget them circumcised from
 their mother.

*.6 But the loss of the ego

.7 gives the ultimate benefit.

54.1   The Master said:

   *.2   Happy are they unattached to material things,

   .3   for yours is the Kingdom of the heavens.

55.1   The Master said:

   *.2   He who does not free himself from attachment
                                to his father and his mother

   .3   will not be able to become my disciple,

   *.4   and he who does not free himself from his brothers
                                      and sisters

   *.5   and does not live every part of his life in my way,

   .6   will not be worthy of me.

56.1   The Master said:

   *.2   He who has found the spiritually dead world

   .3   has found a corpse;

   *.5   and that world is not of worth

   *.4   to him who has found it.

58.1   The Master said:

   *.2   Happy is the man who has toiled to lose the ego,

   .3   he has found the Life.

61 .1   The Master said:

  ★.2   Two, outwardly similar, will rest on a couch, but
being different inwardly

  .3   one will die, the other will live.

  .4   Salome said:

  .5   Is it even as he that is from the One

  .7   that you reclined on my couch

  .8   and ate at my table?

  .9   The Master said to her:

  .10   I am he who is,

  .11   from Him who is the same;

  .12   what belongs to my Father was given to me.

  .13   Salome said: I myself am your disciple.

  .14   Jesus added: Because of that I say this:

  ★.15   When a disciple is emptied, his ego quenched,

  .16   he will be filled with Light;

  ★.17   but when he is divided between his ego and his Self,

  .18   he will be filled with darkness.

62 .1   The Master said:

  .2   I tell my mysteries

  ★.3   to those who are ready to receive my mysteries.

  .4   Whatever your right hand will do,

  .5   let not your left hand be aware

  .6   of what it does.

67 .1 The Master said:

   ★.2 He who would understand the All with his mind,

   ★.3 but if he lacks his true Self

   ★.4 he will be deprived of the All.

69 .1 The Master said:

   .2 Happy are they

   .3 who have been pursued in their hearts.

   .4 It is they

   .5 who have known the Father in Truth.

   ★.6 Happy are they who are hungry for Truth

   ★.7 for the Being of those who desire shall be satisfied.

70 .1 The Master said:

   ★.2 When you bring forth that which is inherently
                                   within yourselves,

   .3 this which is yours will save you;

   ★.4 but if you do not acknowledge that within yourselves,

   ★.5 the invasive ego will kill you, denying access to Truth.

71 .1 The Master said:

   ★.2 I will overturn this domain of duality, doctrines
                       and mental concepts, and the ego,

   ★.3 and no one will be able to build it up again.

74.1 The Master said:
 *.2 There are many thirsting for the water of Life,
 *.3 but nobody immerses himself in the Living water.

75.1 The Master said:
 *.2.3 Many stand, seeking but waiting,
 *.4 but those who stand boldly, prepared to be alone,
 *.5 they shall attain the consummation with Truth.

80.1 The Master said:
 *.2 He who has found the world of objects and thoughts
 .3 has found the body;
 *.5 and that world of objects is of no worth
 *.4 to him who has found it.

81.1 The Master said:
 *.2 He who has become rich spiritually,
 *.3 let him reign;
 *.4 and he who has temporal power,
 .5 let him renounce it!

84 .1 The Master said:

* .2 Seeing your resemblance

* .3 you are accustomed to rejoice.

  .4 But when you will see your images

  .5 that in the beginning were in you,

* .6 which neither die nor are seen now,

* .7 oh! how will you bear the revelation!

87 .1 The Master said:

* .2 Wretched is the person who depends and relies on his
body and mind,

* .3 and wretched is the soul that depends on his person
and his body.

95 .1 The Master said:

  .2 if you have money,

  .3 do not lend at interest,

* .4 but give it away

* .5 to anyone who will not return it.

97.1   The Master said:

.2   The Kingdom of the Father is like a woman

*.3   who started with her full burden of the ego;

*.4   while walking steadily through life

*.6   it gradually dwindled away.

.7   As she did not know it

.8   she could not be troubled by it.

*.9   When she had reached her maturity

*.10   she laid down her burden

*.11   and found the ego gone.

98.1   The Master said:

.2   The Kingdom of the Father is like a man

*.3   wishing to extinguish his ego.

*.4   He summoned his inner strength,

*.5   he tried it out

*.6   in order to be sure his strength would not falter.

*.7   Then he slew his ego.

103.1 The Master said:

  .2 Happy is the man who knows

  *.3 and can discern the wily manifestations of the ego;

  .4 so that he will arise

  .5 and gather his strength

  .6 and prepare for action

  *.7 before they trouble him.

119.1 The Master said:

  *.2 He who knows his spiritual parentage

  *.3 is beyond all worldly wedlock.

106.1 The Master said:

  *.2 When you each make the two One

  *.3 you all will become Sons of man,

  .4 and if you say:

  .5 "Mountain, move away",

  .6 it shall move.

111 .1 The Master said:

*.2 The entire world of objects will become

*.3 unimportant to you,

.4 and he who is living, from the Living,

.5 shall see neither death nor fear,

*.6 because the Master said this:

*.7 For him who finds his true Self

*.8 the world of objects is of no worth.

112 .1 The Master said:

.2 'Woe to the flesh that depends upon the soul!

.3 'Woe to the world that depends upon the flesh!

*.4 Only in Unity is Life to be found.

114 .1 Simon Peter said to them:

.2 Let Mary go out from amongst us,

.3 because women are not worthy of the Life.

*.4 The Master said:

.5 Behold, I will guide her Being

.6 in order that I make her male

*.7,.8 that she like you shall become a living spirit.

*.9 For every person who transcends being woman or man,

.10 shall enter the Kingdom of the heavens.

The Notes

The Notes

0 and 1 Note 1. There is no English word adequate for the Greek word that is presented here as logia. Literally, 'sayings' might be used, but that fails to convey the attitude-changing quality.

0 and 1 Note 2. The Coptic word here for 'hidden' is the same as in logion 109 for the hidden treasure within the field. In the turbulent time of the Master's place and time, it was normal practice to hide treasures thus; and hence they were likely to be found by anyone searching thoroughly.

It would be a great mistake to think of these words to be secret, or esoteric, or for some cult, or only for the initiated. Their inner meanings are treasures, to be manifested to anyone who has the urge to seek them.

1 Note 3. The words 'he who', which occur frequently throughout this Gospel might be rendered 'whoever'. At many places this Teaching emphasizes the spiritual equality of women and men, and is quite specific about this in the last logion.

The important point, however, is that it is in the singular. What is being recorded here attains its real impact when it is regarded as being said to *me*, personally.

1 Note 4. For the strange third phrase it is desirable to consider the Paraphrase. The full meaning of this may wait until reaching logion 19 and its Notes. For the time being, it may be considered as referring to a Life that is unrelated to time (and hence to death) and is therefore attainable as an immediate experience in the here and now.

2 Note 1. In this logion each phrase is self-contained; however, taken together each is of greater inner significance than the one before it. Thus they form a hierarchical sequence, of increasing order.

2 Note 2. In phrases 5 and 6 a Coptic word literally 'to be disturbed or troubled' is here rendered 'turned around' or stirred around. The important thing is that a finder of spiritual Truth *is* turned around—it is much the same idea as in the word metanoia, see Note to logion 28. For any of us it is very disturbing to have to give up our attachment to all the luggage we carry from our material, worldly lives. But that is what the Master is directing us to, and offering to help us, so that we can reach a state of wonderment or marvelling.

3 Note 1. Phrase 2. The Coptic word rendered as

'Being', as here, or as 'heart' in other logia, is very extensible in its meaning. It is used figuratively, and for much more than the seat of love. It is the dynamic centre.

3 Note 2. Phrase 3. A single Coptic word is translated here as 'heaven' or 'sky'. In most instances it is compared or associated with the earth or the sea.

Thus it seems to carry no very specific meaning. In particular, it is important not to attach the figurative meaning – from the Church's doctrine – of the region where God, the saints and the souls of the departed are thought to exist.

3 Note 3. Phrase 7. The Kingdom is not merely within, but it is the inmost part, the core, of each person. It is to be conceived as a condition of Being or living, or as an experience based on sonship of the Father. It may be known here and now. In this context a word has been used that would speak to the Master's Hebrew followers.

Throughout this Teaching the Master is striving to give an awareness of the Kingdom different from that of his hearers. Again, we also need to be careful about attaching preconceived ideas to this word.

3 Note 4. Phrase 8. The Kingdom is also what is outside. More strictly, it is the awareness of the outer world by the inner Being.

Literally: and it is in your exterior.

3 Note 5. Phrases 9 and 10. The verb 'to know' is the key word of this Teaching. It appears in three forms in the Coptic. ϹΟΥⲰΝ is used consistently in this Gospel with the meaning of a profound certainty known at the depth of one's being. It is as when we say "I know that I am myself and no-one else". It is used in logia 3.9, .10, .13, 5.2, 18.9, 19.9, 46.8, 56.2, 65.15, 69.5, 78.8, 80.2, 91.7 and 105.2.

When spelt ϹΟΟⲨⲚ it is used consistently in the Coptic with lesser significance. It is here rendered variously, as 'to realize', 'to recognize', 'to understand', or 'to know' as when we say "I know it is raining". This form occurs in logia 12.2, 16.4, 31.1, 51.8, 65.21, 67.2, 91.8, 103.2, 109.4 and .6.

The third form ⲈΙⲘⲈ is lighter still, and is rendered as 'to be aware', as when we say "I am aware that there are many religions in the world". It occurs in logia 3.11, 21.14, 43.4, 62.5, 97.8 and 98.6 (to be assured).

3 Note 6. Phrases 14 and 15. Literally: then you are in a poverty; and it is you, the poverty.

3 Note 7. It is characteristic of Eastern spiritual books that the author gives at the beginning a concentrated expression of what he has to present; thereafter there are explanations or illustrations to help the reader grasp the essential matter. The example we may be most familiar with is the Prologue to John's Gospel in the Bible.

Here, within the second and third logia, and despite the simple situations, we have the main Teaching of this Gospel: that it is from impoverishment that spirituality releases us, one makes this escape from poverty by seeking, finding, marvelling, coming to know the Self at one's centre, wherein is not only the Kingdom but also the one who reigns over the All.

As one works with this Teaching, becoming more familiar with its concepts, it may be beneficial to turn back to these initial two pages. They will help to retain one on the right path, for much that comes later will be seen to be reflected within the objectives of these opening logia.

4 Note 1.   Not with the mind could we accept that an old man might see the essence of Life in an infant.   But by going to a deeper Place within us the wonder, still unsullied, inherent within each person may be discerned.

4 Note 2.   In the spiritual, whenever two instances—a duality—are recognized, by searching further and going higher a unity may be found.   The commonest experience of this truism is when a man and woman wed, and come to know the Oneness of a marriage.

This Teaching presents examples of such dualities, each of which invites the seeker, by transcending them, to find something higher, a component of Truth.   The first and the last are one such example.

5 This Teaching not only presents the objective of Life but also tells us much about how to reach it.   Here is

the first clue as to the *means* this Teaching is offering for finding spiritual Truth. Phrase 2 was said to the disciples. They could see the Master with their outer eyes, but would need to use their inner Eye to know him; surely the way for us is to try to get that inner Eye working.

7 Note 1. There are ten beatitudes in the Gospel of Thomas, only four of them being also in the Gospels of the Bible. The established term 'blessed' might be used for the Greek word MAKAριος in the original, except that it may carry the implication of being blest by someone outside the man.

The term 'happy' is used here to be consistent with one of the main themes of this Teaching about happiness, joy or bliss; 'joyous' could also be used. These are all pointer-names to it. It is to be found from within, and during this lifetime. Even so, it is necessary to avoid the idea that bliss is to be reserved only for a later life.

7 Note 2. That having been said, it might be well to postpone further consideration of this logion—which has something of the nature of a Zen koan—until the later concept of the ego has been grasped.

When ready for it, recognize that, phrase 4 being the inverse or reverse of phrase 2, our ordinary mental and logical approach would expect phrases 3 and 5 also to be reversed. It is a feature of Eastern spiritual training to challenge that intellectual approach, by making phrases 3 and 5 identical so that the deeper, inner meaning may be found. The clue lies in the awareness that the lion represents the ego; the living Man has assimilated his ego, not been consumed by it.

8 In many spiritual teachings, discrimination is one of the first qualities to be taught. It is partly to permit the useful teaching to be distinguished from the many minor ones; it is partly to avoid reading a wrong interpretation into a teaching—as, at dusk, seeing a snake in a coiled length of rope.

9 We have to till the earth within us beforehand, in order that the words sown by the Master way thrive as a wonderous harvest.

11 Note 1. The heaven and that which is above it relate to a concept at that time that the earth (flat, of course) had a series of layers or hemispheres above it. It is probably adequate to regard the phrase as 'everything'.

11 Note 2. However, this is a difficult logion. It might be prudent to by-pass it initially, and come back to it when more of the ideas of this Teaching have been grasped.

Its phrases relate to the Teaching that each man is originally a Oneness, has developed a duality—largely through the concepts and doctrines of the mind—can come back to the Unity during his life in this world, in which there is no death, and can then purify whatever he assimilates. This can be done by answer to the question: What will you do? It is a quest by the individual.

12 It was James, one of the blood brothers of Jesus, who came in due course to take a leading part amongst the group of disciples of Hebrew background—not yet a Church—that became established in Jerusalem. The final phrase is one that would have been familiar to his Hebrew hearers.

It is implied in this logion that the Master recognized the maturity and capability that was subsequently displayed.

13 Note 1. Together with the records in the Biblical Gospels (Matthew 16:13, Mark 8:27, Luke 9:18) and what can be seen today, this episode may be easily visualized. After his initial ministry around the Lake of Galilee and having gathered some disciples, the Master might have suggested a visit up the River Jordan, 70 kilometres or so through mountainous country, to its source. At that time, as now, merit attached to a journey to the source of a holy river. To accommodate the many pilgrims, Proconsul Hadrian had enhanced a village nearby, in the country of the Phillipians, but by naming it after the Roman Caesar he angered the Jews.

Around the source there have been through the ages small shrines or monuments to sacred figures, philosophers and wise men. At this stage the stature of the Master had not yet been recognized, even by all the disciples. But looking round him he might well have asked whom he resembled. The replies of Peter and Matthew might have been prompted by the small shrines on either hand. However, Thomas had beheld him, with awe and wonder—incomparable.

Immediately, in perhaps an excess of generosity, the Master implied that in a certain sense the experience of Oneness made something common to both the disciple and to the Source.

The source itself of the Jordan is a powerful spring that gushes, bubbling, out of the clefts in the rock at this place. The significance of the dialogue with Thomas that follows is heightened by the newness of the water of the spring, that this spring and the Jordan is the only river in Palestine that flows continuously through the year, and by the immense historical and spiritual importance of the Jordan to anyone born a Jew.

There then develops a situation of a type that is well authenticated: a Master can discern the spiritual capability of a follower, and, taking him aside, gives a facet of Truth that others are not yet ready to grasp. There is not much likelihood that the others would wish to record this. Furthermore, that Truth that was communicated was considered a blasphemy—punishable by ritual stoning—by one of a Hebrew background; how could anyone other than he who had this daunting experience recount it, or feel it important to record it, and consider that it has the power to be a consuming fire? It can only be looked on as the 'coded signature' by Thomas to his Gospel.

13 Note 2. Phrase 2. Literally: Compare me.
Phrases 9 and 10. Literally: Master, my mouth will absolutely reject / that I say: you resemble whom.
Phrase 14. Literally the word for 'being drunk' is used; here it refers to the initial stage as when we say "I was intoxicated by the beauty of the sunset". The same word when used in logion 28.11 relates to the second stage of being in a state of dull inebriation.
Phrases 16 and 17. Literally: And he took him, he withdrew.

15 To behold Him who was not begotten is to see Him with the inner Eye—as in logion 5.

16 Note 1. The word presented here by the colloquial term 'loners' has been translated elsewhere as 'solitaries' or solitary ones. But there is no call in this Teaching to the life of the hermit. There is also a related colloquial term 'outsiders' but there is no call to shun contacts with others. The intended idea, which appears in several contexts, is that one bent on finding spiritual Truth should not expect merely to ride along with the herd, but may have to be prepared at the spiritual level to go out independently of other people, to be unattached, to stand up as an individual with courage and boldness.
Also, see Note 1 for logion 49.

16 Note 2. The Coptic word in phrase 5 carries a sense of a positive type of division, a discrimination—to separate light and darkness, heavenly and material, good and evil; perhaps as fire separates gold from dross.

18 Note 1. The Master answers a question about death by directing us to become aware of our beginning. The logia in this Teaching are a whole. So look elsewhere for that. Logia 19, 50, 49 and 4 (in that order) reiterate that in our beginning we come from the Light; it is inherent within us, and by seeing it we come to a Life in the here and now that is independent of the death of the body.

Thus to know rightly the beginning and the end leads to living in the present, and concern about death does not arise.

18 Note 2. Phrases 8 to 10. Throughout, 'shall' is used not only as the future tense, but also with its legitimate coloration of promise or assurance. This derives from its early English usage of being a command. Thus on each occasion the reader may feel a sense of authority, certainty and conviction.

19 Note 1. Logia 18 and 19 deal with the happiness of knowing that one's true identity exists throughout life. It is there at the beginning (logion 4 spoke of that) and extends to the end. However, it is more than a continuity within time; more specifically the real Self is independent of time.

Such Life is not merely immortal, but rather is outside of the concept of time, and so is independent of death.

Phrases 2 and 3 of this logion are a prompt to take us to an awareness of an even higher level than the previous logion. Whereas that directed us to disregard the beginning and the end—a duality—this refers to finding what was and is as a Oneness. The logia heard and known inwardly by the disciple make a happy man, their stone-like words are raised to become living ministry, the trees of completeness are changeless through the seasons, and he tastes not death.

19 Note 2. Phrase 7. The five trees in Paradise represent man in his primary and essential purity. Five, for him to be complete in his five members. Not to be confused with the tree of life, nor the tree in the Garden of Eden.

Phrase 8. Literally: which are unmoved in summer or winter.

20 There is no hint that the word 'heavens' differs significantly from the word 'heaven', nor that the 'Kingdom of the heavens' differs from the 'Kingdom'.

21 Note 1. In this Teaching the 'robbers' are the forces within us that steal away our awareness of what is truly within—they live in the ego. This wily ego can appear in many different forms—making us dwell in a field not really ours, as an outward façade, as a thief, as a brigand—that demand one's strength to overcome.

21 Note 2. Phrase 10. Literally: They strip themselves naked before them.
Phrase 21. Literally: gird up your loins with great strength. Also in logion 103.6.

22 Note 1. This is one of the great logia, if only because it can lead us through progressively higher levels of awareness. It is a saying worth returning to, even over a period of years.

It starts with simple questions, where the Master was amongst those, accustomed to the Hebrew idiom, who had at least discerned the unsullied quality in each of us as children (logia 4, 18, 19 and 21). The Master responds in characteristically Semitic speech, yet by phrase 9 it has become necessary to move to the Greek idiom to provide the answers. Amongst the many instances of two becoming One, Unity found from duality, that in phrase 9 refers—as so often in this Teaching—to the ego and the Self within each of us.

By phrase 14 maleness and femaleness have merged, or risen to a stage for which we have the word mankind. This is amplified or confirmed in phrases 15 and 16, where both the male and the female have disappeared. Perhaps it might have been the wish of the Master that those who cry for feminism would rise to this level.

Throughout this saying the rhythm of every one of the short phrases places the emphasis, the key-point, at the end of the phrase. So in phrase 17 we have to convert out physical eyes into our third or inner spiritual eye, and in the three following phrases by going beyond the mind the tangible hand, foot or even image is raised to the intangible or spiritual form.

Finally the Master shows that this traverse of high spiritual Teaching can come back to the Hebrew summit.

22 Note 2. Phrase 20. Philo, in Platonic fashion, expresses the thought that first of all an image of the Father proceeded from him which, in turn, served as an image or pattern (as in casting) for man. The term 'image' (Greek ΕΙΚШΝ) used here and in logia 50, 83 and 84 relates to this concept.

22 Note 3. In the Coptic, three different future tenses are used. In phrases 6 and 21, something will simply happen. In 13 there is a greater emphasis and a sense of an enduring condition. Moreover, in 10, 11 and 17 the emphasis and state of permanence is even greater.

22 Note 4. Phrases 17 to 20. Literally: ...in the place of...

24 Exceptionally, 'Light', 'illumines' and 'shine' are used here for one Coptic word.

27 Note 1. Phrase 1. The word 'abstain', Greek ΝΗϚΤΕγШ,

has here a positive connotation, compared with its use in other logia as 'to fast' (and associated with prayer). It denotes a discrimination, whereby the world of objects may be transcended. Nevertheless, the objective world is not to be rejected, but rather it is to be accepted and the spiritual life is to be lived within it.

Elsewhere, words are attributed to Jesus: "I am *in* the world, but I am not *of* the world". It is this relationship of the objective and spiritual worlds—seeing the former from the right position, and making it point towards the latter—that has great efficacy.

27 Note 2. Phrase 3. To make of the sabbath a true sabbath—an interior attainment in contrast to the external observation of the Law in keeping the sabbath—is to behold the Father.

Literally: if you make not of the sabbath, the sabbath.

28 Note 1. Phrase 13. To transform one's knowing is a direct rendering of the Greek word ΜΕΤΑΝΟΙΑ— important in this and the Biblical Gospels, although regrettably often translated as 'to repent', which leads us off in all sorts of wrong directions. Even the phrase to transform one's knowing is inadequate; it is rather a transformation of one's awareness, a change that comes about as a result of a new view-point.

Thus this knowing means more than just an understanding with the mind. It is a word, acting as a noun, derived from the word 'to know' when that is carrying its primary and deepest meaning, as mentioned in Note 6 of logion 3.

28 Note 2.   In this Teaching to be empty is to be free from the dominance of the ego.

34 To guide the Being of any person is a concept worthy of a Master.

35 In this, the first logion to deal specifically with the ego, it is made clear that we need first to become aware of the ego, to be able to control its workings.

37 Shame, pride, ostentation and outward façades are all manifestations of the ego.   To strip oneself of them and trample them *automatically* reveals the Self, in which there is no fear.

40 Phrase 2.   Literally: A vine was planted in the place outside of the Father.

42 Here a Master distils and crystallizes the expression

of a facet of Truth—its brevity precludes all dross. In the original it comprises only three words: the Coptic verb 'to become' in the imperative tense, implying an assertion or promise; the pronoun 'you' in the plural; and the Greek verb ΠΑρΑΓω 'to pass away' in the circumstantial present tense rendered into English with a participle or 'while'.

The hand-written form gives the nearest direct rendering. A more liberal translation might be 'Become, as passers by' or even 'Become passers-by'. An expanded rendering is 'Become your true Selves, as your egos pass away'.

The intent is to prompt us—it is in the imperative —to disregard the things of the material world or of our minds and emotions, to become unattached to them. Thus, for example, to do all the outward things of living without being a 'doer'; or when troubles beset us to let them pass by; or to allow the good and pleasing things to come to us without in any way claiming them. All such attachment, or being a doer, or claiming comes from the ego. Letting the dominance of that go, we become our real Selves.

46 Note 1. John was sufficiently clear-sighted to have the potential to recognize, at some future date, the Truth presented by the Master in his maturity. But anyone around the Master, by dropping his ego, shall know it actually rather than potentially.

This logion implies that John was living when it was spoken, so it would have come from early in Jesus' ministry.

46 Note 2.   Phrase 5.   Literally: so that his eyes will not be broken.

47 Here seven word-pictures all refer to the way of the Master being superior to the old, and that the two will not mix.   He was offering them new light.

Phrases 9, 10 and 14, 15 relate to wine that has deteriorated by being kept too long in wineskins.

In phrase 18 the Coptic word for 'new' (in this phrase) implies also a better quality.

In phrase 19 the word 'a division' here carries the meaning of the modern term 'a mismatch'.

48 In this Teaching a house refers to the Being of man. The ego and the real Self need to make peace with each other.

49 Note 1.   There is no English word for the Greek word MONAχOϚ rendered here by the colloquial term 'loners'.   However, in this logion, particularly, it may also carry the meaning of 'they that have found the Oneness'.

See Note 1 for logion 16, and also Note for logion 75.

49 and **50**   Note 2.   The word 'chosen' should here, as in the Bible, carry the sense of being separated rather than being favoured.

50 Note 2. At phrase 8 the manuscript is damaged, being at a corner of a page. It has been reconstructed as 'It stood up'. For the next phrase see the Note to logion 5.

51 A cardinal feature of this Teaching is that the true Life can be found and known during this life, rather than being only in some life after death or in a messianic future or at the millennium.

52 The Master contrasts the views of his disciples, that the revelations of the Prophets are what is significant, with the living word he is giving them.

53 The Master is telling the disciples not to dwell on what the Prophets, who were dead, foretold but to be in his living presence before them. (See logion 5.)

55 To 'turn away from' is a rather free translation of the Coptic verb in phrases 2 and 5 (and its Greek form ΜΙϬΕΟ), which has no English equivalent to give its right flavour; it is a contrast with 'to love', for which we would need to invent a word 'to dis-love'. In other logia

word, and the Greek word monakhos (MONAχOς , in logia 16, 49 and 75), and also the more recent term 'non- attachment' all point to the same concept.

Phrase 5. Literally: does not bear his cross...

57 Note 1.   Phrase 2.   The Kingdom of the Father seems to be indistinguishable from the Kingdom.

57 Note 2.   In phrases 3 and 5 we would say seedling crop, one that has begun to grow, not merely the grain.

57 Note 3.   Phrase 6 is literally '. . . allow them to pull up . . .'   It has been suggested that a sentence has been omitted between phrases 5 and 6.

62 Note 1.   'Mystery' (Greek MγςTHρION) does not here mean something mysterious, but the inner meaning of a saying.

62 Note 2.   To make the two One is to abolish the subject-object distinction.   The left hand can only know what the right hand is doing through the intermediary of the mind.   By going beyond the mind it is reduced to silence and is suppressed; then there is simply a pure attention, without judgement on the right hand's action.   By this example, the Master teaches us how we must receive his mysteries.

65 There are an appreciable number of logia in which the disciples or other listeners had come with pre-suppositions or had failed to understand the Master, and he works to correct their awareness. There are a few (59, 74, 86, 91, 92 and 117) in which he can only challenge them to rise to something better. But in this and the following logion he seems almost to have despaired of some of his people—parables of rejection and even killing.

Let anyone who seeks be not amongst that category.

67 This logion is like a Zen koan or 'non-statement' —typical of an oriental Teacher. It tries to take the seeker beyond his logical mind, to a higher level within. The Paraphrase takes some of the steps along this path. And note that the knowing of the Self precedes the knowing of the All.

Literally the final phrase is 'is in want of the All-place.'

68 The word ΔΙωΚω is used in classical Greek, and sometimes in the Bible, with meanings to hasten, run after, pursue, strive for, seek after, follow eagerly, etc. It is noteworthy that in the Bible, but not elsewhere, it is used for persecute; it may be as though the writers of the New Testament adapted the word to deal with the sufferings that had by then befallen Christians.

It is used here, in phrases 4 and 5 and in logion 69.3, in its earlier sense; anyway, the context requires it. To be detached and pursued in the heart gives the urge to find Truth.

For 'heart' see Note 1 to logion 3.

For 'dislike' see Paraphrase of logion 55.

70 There is equivalence between this logion and logion 4 with its destructive lion.

71 To 'overturn this house' is very similar to the 'being turned around' of logion 2. But the following phrase requires the deeper meaning given in the Paraphrase.

75 Note 1. The word 'loners' is used here with the meaning given in Note 1 for logion 16.

75 Note 2. Phrase 5. Literally: who shall enter the place of the marriage.

77 In phrases 6 to 9, this is not the pantheistic doctrine that there is divinity in a piece of wood or stone, but an encouragement that the world of objects may, when rightly viewed, point us to the Ultimate.

78 To regard this as a call to the life of an ascetic is only to see the first level of meaning. It is the final phrase that directs us towards non-attachment to worldly things.

79 Note 1. It is possible that this logion in its entirety may be a reflection of the attitude, prevalent at that time and place, of an apocalypse to befall the people. It is equally possible, however, that the last three phrases may have been added within the severely ascetic community—known technically as an encratitic movement—in which the Gospel as we have it now was probably written down. It is one of the few examples of such possible coloration.

79 Note 2. Phrase 5. Here the Greek word Logos is used, which is sometimes, but inadequately, rendered as Word. 'To have grasped the Divine Meaning' comes somewhere near to conveying the sense here.

80 Logia 56 and 80 are nearly identical, except for two Greek words rendered as corpse and body; but there seems little difference between them.

83 and **84** In this Teaching the Master sees each person to be born in a state of perfection (logia 19, 46 and 50), which could be referred to by the phrases 'primordial image' or the 'original pattern'. We lapse from this perfection, and the spiritual work is to come to know it again (logia 49 and 70). `

The Paraphrase for 84 is given to help with this difficult logion.

The concept of images is one of the more sophisticated in this Teaching, and can only be dealt with in an essay.

88 His Hebrew hearers were accustomed to the angels and the prophets, and knew what they could give. However, the Master asserts that this is also possessed by the disciples. He wishes them to become aware of it, and to ask the question that will lead to knowing that these two are One.

89 For this to be a call to maintain a life of both an inner and an outer purity is again only to see the first level of meaning. The inside and the outside represent a duality, and a key teaching throughout this Gospel is that whenever a duality is identified there is need to seek further for a Unity above or beyond both. Ask oneself what the pronoun points towards.

90 Phrase 3. The term 'yoke' may be related to 'yoga', which is best understood as 'spiritual discipline'. It does not mean 'burden'.

91 This is the only occurrence, in phrase 3, of the word 'believe', and it is used by disciples from the Hebrew background. In this Teaching, the Master never uses nor refers to the concept of belief, or of believing, or of believers.

Likewise, nowhere in this Teaching is there reference to faith, to having faith, to being one of the faithful.

Instead, the key concept of the Teaching is to know—spiritual Truth being something that is found and known.

The final phrase is a challenge to take us to logion 5.

92 The final phrase is a challenge to take us to logion 2, and to find the assurance of logion 94.

93 As in other spiritual Teachings, the great treasures are only for those prepared to receive them. This comes also in logia 16, 23, 49 and 50.

94 Phrase 3. Literally: and he who knocks within, it will be opened to him.

95 Literally: Jesus said: If you have monies, do not lend at interest, but give [them] to him from whom you will not receive them.

99 Literally: Those who are in these places, who do the wish of my Father.

100 This is the only reference in this Teaching to God as the word is used in the Hebrew and Biblical scriptures.

Here in phrases 5 to 7 is another hierarchical sequence of phrases, of increasing order. The conclusion to be drawn is startling.

101 For the verb in phrase 1, see the Note for logion 55.

103 The manifestations of the ego—the robbers—are wily, creeping up on us from all directions, all unexpected.

Phrase 6. Literally: gird up your loins with great strength.

107 The wise fisherman, near the start of these Teachings (logion 8), could discern and distinguish the large from the small. Here, as we approach the finish, the shepherd desires the Oneness that leads to the Kingdom.

108 The full impact of this logion will be felt when it is combined with the great affirmation of the first four phrases of logion 77. The ultimate promise.

109 Note 1. Any man may own a field, bequeath it to his son, and unknowingly it may be sold. The Kingdom is for those who find the treasure that all along is hidden within, waiting to be found.

109 Note 2. Phrase 10. Finding the hidden meanings of these logia (see Note for logion 2) is not a trivial task or a matter of chance. Work has to be done inwardly in a diligent and systematic manner to find Truth at this level.

109 Note 3. Phrase 7. Literally: he took the field there.

112 The flesh and the soul are a duality; so are the soul and the flesh. Within each, the two elements are linked by the mind. To be centred in the mind is a woeful state.

By putting both phrases in juxtaposition, with something like a Zen koan, the Master seeks to raise us beyond the mind, to the Place where the Being is in Oneness.

114 This final logion, together with many others (3, 6, 12, 14, 16, 18, 20, 22, 24, 37, 43, 51, 53, 78, 91, 99 and 117), has two characteristic elements. First, they relate to live situations, which may encourage us to regard them as authentic. Secondly, the Master speaks contrary to the disciples' presuppositions; he is seeking to open their eyes from a blindness, to awaken their awareness of the Truth he is giving. Is there any possibility that we too may have presuppositions to which his words might apply?

In this logion we have such a simple start—dear Simon Peter speaking out brashly again and with male chauvinism that was so deeply ingrained in those days.

The Master asserts that he will guide Mary's Being (logion 34 and its Note), to become a living spirit. As in the Paraphrase, the emphasis is not on the maleness—even the males have to be guided to become living spirits. Women are not being asked to resemble men, but we are all being directed to that level of Reality where the objective woman and the objective male cease to exist. It is exactly the same as the highest stage of logion 22, and it is the entry to the Kingdom.

★   ★   ★   ★   ★

So here we can see that this is no mosaic, no mere collection of sayings culled from different sources. It is a harmonious, homogeneous Teaching, its elements linked together like pieces of a jig-saw or the coloured tufts in a patterned carpet. Its various components, all expressed in the symbolic language of parable that has the power to reach directly to the Being within, help to explain and provide the route to attain the objectives set out in the two opening pages. It is from spiritual poverty that we can be taken. This is to be done by a reciprocal knowing of the Self, to reach the Kingdom wherein there is the possibility to reign over the All. At that Ultimate there can be nothing further, just tranquil joy and happiness exists.

References and Acknowledgements

The following earlier translations of the Gospel of Thomas were especially valuable in preparing this translation. The extreme value of the pioneering work by the French scholars of L'Association Métanoïa is gratefully acknowledged.

The Gospel According to Thomas by A Guillaumont, H-Ch Puech, G Quispel, W Till and Yassah 'Abd Al Masīh. Published 1959 and 1976 by E Brill, Leyden, Holland

L'Évangile Selon Thomas by Phillipe de Suarez. Published 1975 by Association Métanoïa, 26200, Montelimar, France

Évangile Selon Thomas by É Gillabert, P Bourgeois and Y Haas. Published 1979 by Association Métanoïa

The Nag Hammâdi Library in English edited by J M Robinson, translated by T O Lambdin. Published by E J Brill